Rihanna

By Robin Johnson

Crabtree Publishing Company

www.crabtreebooks.com

Crabtree Publishing Company
www.crabtreebooks.com

Author: Robin Johnson
Publishing plan research and development:
Sean Charlebois, Reagan Miller
Crabtree Publishing Company
Coordinating editor: Paul Humphrey
Editors: Colleen Ruck, Kathy Middleton,
Jessica Shapiro
Proofreader: Shannon Welbourn
Photo researcher: Colleen Ruck
Series and cover design: Ken Wright
Layout: Ian Winton
**Production coordinator and
prepress technician:** Ken Wright
Print coordinators: Katherine Berti,
Margaret Amy Salter

Photographs:
Alamy: AF Archive/Alamy: page 15; Alamy
Celebrity: page 7, 23; ZUMA Wire Service/
Alamy: page 17
Bigstock: Kath Click: page 18
Corbis: Mike Black/Reuters: page 16;
Splash News: page 9
Getty Images: Evan Agostini: page 14; Jeff
Kravitz/AMA 2010: page 25; Kevin
Mazur/Contributor: page 19; NBAE/
Getty Images: page 23
Keystone Press: © BIG Pictures UK: cover
Photoshot: Everett: page 12; Retna/
Photoshot: page 24
Rex Features: David Crichlow: page 8(b);
Greg Allen: page 20; Star Traks Photo:
pages 11 (t), 28; Rex Features: pages 18, 21, 26
Shutterstock: Feature Flash: title page, 5;
Shelly Wall: page 6; Holger W: page 8 (t);
Adam J. Sablich: pages 10, 13; Joe Seer:
page 27
Wikimedia Commons: pages 4, 5, 11 (b), 22

Produced for Crabtree Publishing Company
by Discovery Books

Library and Archives Canada Cataloguing in Publication

Johnson, Robin (Robin R.)
Rihanna / Robin Johnson.

(Superstars!)
Includes index.
Issued also in electronic formats.
ISBN 978-0-7787-1051-6 (bound).--ISBN 978-0-7787-1055-4 (pbk.)

1. Rihanna, 1988- --Juvenile literature. 2. Singers--Barbados--
Biography--Juvenile literature. 3. Singers--United States--
Biography--Juvenile literature. I. Title. II. Series: Superstars!
(St. Catharines, Ont.)

ML3930.R568J68 2013   j782.42164092   C2013-900436-X

Library of Congress Cataloging-in-Publication Data

Johnson, Robin (Robin R.)
Rihanna / by Robin Johnson.
pages ; cm. -- (Superstars!)
Includes index.
ISBN 978-0-7787-1051-6 (reinforced library binding) --
ISBN 978-0-7787-1055-4 (pbk.) -- ISBN 978-1-4271-9301-8
(electronic pdf) -- ISBN 978-1-4271-9225-7 (electronic html)
1. Rihanna, 1988---Juvenile literature. 2. Singers--Biography--
Juvenile literature. I. Title.

ML3930.R44J64 2013
782.42164092--dc23
[B]

2013001650

Crabtree Publishing Company

www.crabtreebooks.com   1-800-387-7650

Printed in the USA/052013/JA20130412

Published in Canada
Crabtree Publishing
616 Welland Ave.
St. Catharines, ON
L2M 5V6

Published in the United States
Crabtree Publishing
PMB 59051
350 Fifth Avenue, 59th Floor
New York, New York 10118

Published in the United Kingdom
Crabtree Publishing
Maritime House
Basin Road North, Hove
BN41 1WR

Published in Australia
Crabtree Publishing
3 Charles Street
Coburg North
VIC, 3058

CONTENTS

Words that are defined in the glossary are in
bold type the first time they appear in the text.

Rated Rihanna

Rihanna is a sassy singing sensation. The beauty from Barbados burst onto the music scene in 2005. Since then, the talented young singer has pumped out seven smash studio albums. Selling more than 30 million records, Rihanna has toured the globe performing her hit songs for sold-out crowds. And she does it all with superstar style.

RAH-RAH FOR RIRI!

Rihanna's nickname is "RiRi." Her friends and family call her "Robyn," which is the singer's real first name. (Rihanna is her middle name.)

Rihanna is a powerful pop music machine.

Singles Lady

Rihanna released her first single at the age of 17. "Pon de Replay" was a lively pop tune that got everyone dancing. It also got people talking about the hot new **R&B** singer. Two years later, Rihanna shared her song "Umbrella" with the world. It rocketed the singer to the top of the charts and made her famous around the world. Rihanna has seven albums to her credit and 11 number one singles under her bejeweled belt.

PERFECT 10

Rihanna produced 10 number-one singles in less than five years! That's faster than any other solo artist in history. Rihanna is also the youngest artist ever to have 10 songs hit the top spot. She did so by the age of 23.

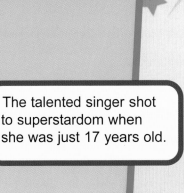

The talented singer shot to superstardom when she was just 17 years old.

Singing Her Praises

Rhianna is a **versatile** performer who's music ranges from pop and rock to rap, R&B, and soul. She has been honored with more than 100 awards for her albums, singles, and videos. The striking singer has also won awards for her fashion, her acting—and even her legs!

Fierce Fashionista

Famous for her stunning good looks, the 5′8″ (173 cm) one-time beauty queen constantly changes her appearance. She has rocked more than 150 different hairstyles since she began making music! Rihanna sports daring outfits in concerts and on red-carpet runways. Her fierce fashions are designed to shock and wow her fans—and they work!

Rihanna can easily transform from a fresh-faced Caribbean beauty to a fearless tattooed rocker.

I think my best quality is being daring and spontaneous. Risky. Fearless.
—Interview in *Elle* magazine, May 2012

RihannaNavy

Rihanna's fans are called RihannaNavy. They are a navy of hardcore fans that have been recruited since 2005. More than 28 million follow Rihanna on Twitter and more than 66 million like her on Facebook.

A young member of RihannaNavy shows her support.

*We're **peers**. They're right here with me. I need them more than they need me. I need their feedback, I need their honesty, and I need their support. Without that, it's pointless. I respect them very, very much.*
—Rihanna discussing her fans, in *Glamour* magazine, September 2011

Music of the Sun

Rihanna grew up in Barbados, an island in the Caribbean Sea south of the United States. It is known for being a popular destination for tourists because of its hot climate and beautiful beaches. Today, the island is also known for one of its most famous citizens—Rihanna!

Barbados is a small country with a population of about 287,000 people.

Born in Barbados

Robyn Rihanna Fenty was born on February 20, 1988, in Saint Michael, Barbados. She grew up in a small house in the city of Bridgetown. Rihanna lived with her parents and younger brothers, Rorrey and Rajad. Her mother, Monica, was an accountant. Her father, Ronald, ran a clothing warehouse.

Rihanna also has two half-sisters and one half-brother. Her sister Samantha and father helped her celebrate the launch of her album.

Summer all Year Round

Rihanna thought growing up in Barbados was perfect. The beach was her playground everyday in the tropical climate.

Rihanna enjoys jet-skiing in Barbados.

She Said It

[My first name,] Robyn, is the brick to my foundation. It's something I hold on to. It's everything I grew up with, my childhood, Barbados, people close to me. Everything that's familiar. People know Rihanna from my music. But if this were to all go away tomorrow, I would always look at myself as Robyn.

—Rihanna discussing her name in *Rolling Stone* magazine, April 2011

From Shy to Fly

Rihanna started singing around the age of seven. She loved to sing and dance, but was very shy and did not perform in public. Rihanna entertained her family, friends, and neighbors, though. She also sang to herself to get through tough times. Growing up, she suffered from terrible headaches. There was also **turmoil** in her family. Rihanna's father was **addicted** to drugs and alcohol. Her parents fought often, then divorced when Rihanna was 14 years old.

Rihanna has always loved to sing and dance.

She Said It

[My father] taught me how to fish, how to swim, how to run, how to ride. He really toughened me up.
—Rihanna discussing her father in *Rolling Stone* magazine, April 2011

10

Girl Group

At the age of 15, Rihanna formed a girl group with two of her friends. They performed the Mariah Carey song "Hero" in a school talent show. They won the contest. Not long after the show she met American record producer Evan Rogers through family friends. Rogers was on vacation in Barbados and asked her to audition.

GIRL POWER

Growing up, Rihanna was **influenced** by such legendary performers as Mariah Carey, Destiny's Child, Whitney Houston, Celine Dion, and Madonna.

Rihanna won a high school beauty pageant at the age of 15.

Mariah Carey is one of Rihanna's biggest influences.

Something Special

Rihanna **auditioned** for Rogers with her friends. He fell instantly in love with their sweet and funky Caribbean pop sound. But mostly Rogers saw something special in the talented young singer. He **signed** Rihanna and invited her to the United States to start making music. Rihanna left her home in Barbados to find stardom in America.

Jamming for Def Jam

In December 2003, Rihanna moved to Stamford, Connecticut, and lived with her producer and his wife. She recorded a four-song **demo tape**, which Rogers sent to a number of record **labels**. It soon caught the attention of Shawn "Jay-Z" Carter. A superstar rapper, Jay-Z was also president of Def Jam Recordings. In February 2005, Rihanna auditioned for Jay-Z in New York. That same day, she signed a deal with Def Jam to record six albums!

When she auditioned for Jay-Rihanna sang "Pon de Replay" and Whitney Houston's "For the Love of You."

He Said It

She was obviously nervous. Now she has a big personality, but I didn't get that in the meeting. What I did get was her eyes, this determination. She was fierce... I knew she was a star.

—Jay-Z describing Rihanna's audition, in *Rolling Stone* magazine, April 2011

Sunny Skies Ahead

Rihanna released her **debut** album on August 12, 2005. *Music of the Sun* was a bubbly mix of R&B, reggae, and pop. The album was instantly hot! It went gold, selling more than 500,000 copies.

Instant Replay

The album's debut single—"Pon de Replay"—was Rihanna's first big hit. The title of the song means "play it again" in Bajan Creole, one of Barbados' two languages. Young fans did replay the song… again and again! In fact, "Pon de Replay" shot all the way to number two on the U.S. *Billboard* Hot 100 chart.

Rihanna performs her hit debut single "Pon de Replay" at the 2005 Monster Jam.

She Said It

In the beginning of my career, it was really strict for me. I couldn't wear pink or red lipstick; it was just bizarre. We had a young fan base, and they were trying to keep me fresh. But I just really wanted to be myself. I wanted to be sassy, the attitude, all these things that I am.
—Interview in *Glamour* magazine, September 2011

A Girl Like Me

Rihanna returned to the studio just a month after her first record was released. She got right to work recording new tracks for her second album. *A Girl Like Me* was released in April 2006, less than eight months later. "SOS"—the album's first single—soared to the top of the charts. It reached the number one spot on the *Billboard* Hot 100 and stayed there for three straight weeks.

Rihanna accepts a platinum record plaque for her album *A Girl Like Me* on NBC's *Today Show*.

On the Road

In the summer of 2006, Rihanna hit the road to **promote** her first two albums. The month-long Rihanna: Live in Concert Tour was the first **headlining** tour for the young singer. She performed 20 shows in the United States, Canada, and Jamaica. Rihanna impressed audiences with her powerful voice and smooth dance moves.

Three Cheers for Rihanna!

Later that summer, Rihanna brought her acting talents to the comedy *Bring It On: All or Nothing*. In the film, two rival cheerleading squads compete for a chance to appear in Rihanna's latest music video. She had a small **cameo** role playing herself in the film. The cheerleading movie gave the singer a taste for acting.

Bring It On: All or Nothing proved that Rihanna could act as well as sing.

She Said It

For me acting was a whole different world. We make mini-movies with music videos but there is always a song track that is playing. You don't have to speak. With acting you have to tell that emotion with the tone of your voice. This isn't my first career choice. I think it is always going to be a challenge for me, but I like that.
—Interview with MTV, May 2012

Good Girl Gone Bad

Rihanna's first two albums made her famous around the world. The ambitious singer did not stop for long to enjoy her newfound success, however. Rihanna got back in the studio and began recording her third album.

Rihanna Reloaded

Good Girl Gone Bad hit stores in May 2007. A year later, the album was released again as *Good Girl Gone Bad: Reloaded* with three extra songs. The upbeat dance-pop record was Rihanna's biggest and best-selling album—so far. It stayed on the *Billboard*

200 list for nearly 100 weeks and sold millions of copies around the world. *Good Girl Gone Bad* received a whopping nine Grammy Award nominations! Rihanna ended up winning the Grammy for Best Rap/Sung **Collaboration** with Jay-Z for her hit song "Umbrella."

Rihanna and Jay-Z accept a Grammy Award for their hit song "Umbrella."

She Said It

When I won the first Grammy, there was no other feeling like that feeling. It just made me feel like I came so far, like that was just a dream a few years before that, and then it was happening right then. I went to the Grammys that year just to watch. I didn't even think we'd win. So that surprised me.
—*Interview* magazine, December 2010

Don't Stop the Singles

Rihanna released seven more singles from *Good Girl Gone Bad*. Most of them were hits. "Don't Stop the Music" was a popular upbeat song that danced its way to the third spot on the *Billboard* Hot 100— and a Grammy nomination. "Take a Bow" and "Disturbia" both reached the top of the charts. The singles "Hate That I Love You," "If I Never See Your Face Again," and "Disturbia" were all nominated for Grammy Awards.

World Tour

In September 2007, Rihanna hit the road to promote her third album. The Good Girl Gone Bad Tour was the singer's first world concert tour. Rihanna toured for 16 months and performed 80 shows across five continents. The singer wowed fans with her strong vocals and **elaborate** sets. She also shocked many people with her barely-there leather outfits.

The tour showed the world that Rihanna was a talented performer.

17

Rumors, Relationships, and Rivalry

Rihanna also makes headlines in her personal life, although often for circumstances beyond her control. Rumors have swirled over the years that she had a romantic relationship with her mentor, Jay-Z. Both she and Jay-Z have always dismissed the rumors as ridiculous. She has also been linked with actors Ashton Kutcher and Robert Pattinson, as well as rapper Drake, with whom she has worked. Rihanna knows that people are interested in her love life, but she says that it is one of those things that should not matter to anyone else.

In fact, Jay-Z's wife Beyoncé and Rihanna are friends. Rihanna has insisted that she does not regard Beyoncé as a music rival. She is a big fan of the former Destiny's Child star and enjoys her music. "She is definitely not the enemy, it is not a competition. I love her, I love her so much." Rihanna told U.S. radio station WENN.

Beyoncé and Rihanna are sometimes seen as rivals in the industry, but they are friends.

Dangerous Love

Although everything in Rihanna's music life was going well, her personal life suddenly took a turn for the worse in February 2009. Rihanna was **assaulted** by her boyfriend, American R&B star Chris Brown. The pair had been dating for two years. One night, the couple argued in Brown's car and he attacked her. The attack left Rihanna bruised and bloody. Brown pleaded guilty to assault and was sentenced to five years' **probation**. Rihanna has called this period a confusing time in her life. The assault ended their relationship.

Rihanna and Chris Brown attend an awards ceremony in Beverley Hills before the assault.

She Said It

It happened to me and it happened to me in front of the world. It was embarrassing, it was humiliating, it was hurtful... I lost my best friend. Everything I knew switched in a night...

—Interview with Oprah Winfrey, August 2012

Talking Tough

After the assault, Rihanna was sad, angry, and confused. She says it was the hardest time of her life. The singer refused to show her pain and did not want people's sympathy. Instead, Rihanna began talking and acting tough. She got a tattoo of a small gun under her arm. She also expressed her anger in her fourth album, *Rated R*.

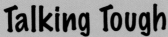

THINK INK

Rihanna has tattoos from head to toe! She got her first ink—a set of music notes on her right foot—when she was 18 years old. Since then, Rihanna has added stars, a cross, a skull with a pink hair bow, a number of messages, and many other tattoos to her body.

Rihanna has said she likes to study tattoo "culture."

Rated R

Rated R was released on November 20, 2009. Unlike Rihanna's first three albums, Rated R was dark, emotional, and edgy. Rihanna sang about abuse, gangsters, guns, murder, and revenge. Like her first three albums, Rated R was a success. Just as she did when she was younger, she used music to get her through tough times. The song "Rude Boy" topped the charts. Rihanna performed the hit songs on The Last Girl on Earth Tour.

RAPPING PRESENTS

In July 2009, Rihanna joined rappers Jay-Z and Kanye West on the single "Run This Town." The trio earned two Grammy Awards for the hit rap song. A year later, Rihanna collaborated with rapper Eminem on the song "Love the Way You Lie." The pair were nominated for three Grammy Awards, including Song of the Year.

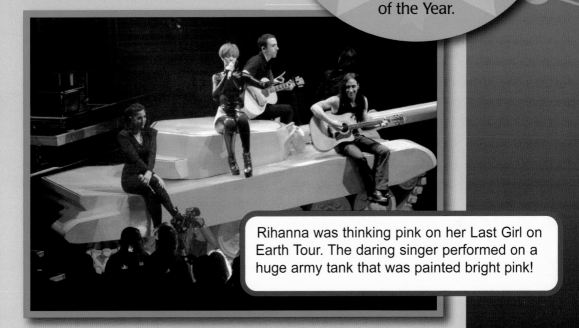

Rihanna was thinking pink on her Last Girl on Earth Tour. The daring singer performed on a huge army tank that was painted bright pink!

She Said It

Rated R *was the album that became really real, very honest. After that, it's hard to go back to doing songs that are fiction. There was no coming back.*
—Interview in *Glamour* magazine, September 2011

Rihanna Gets Loud

Rihanna released her fifth record, called *Loud*, in November 2010. The singer returned to her upbeat pop, dance, and R&B roots on the album. Three singles from *Loud* reached the top spot on the charts. Rihanna won a Grammy Award for Best Dance Recording for the single "Only Girl." She launched the lively Loud Tour in the summer of 2011 to promote her hit album.

She Said It

I feel like it was a really fun, expressive album, and loud was the perfect word to symbolize that.
—Rihanna discussing *Loud* in *Interview* magazine, December 2010

Talk That Talk

Rihanna released her sixth album at the end of 2011. *Talk That Talk* burst onto the *Billboard* 200 chart in third place. Fans loved the album's debut single, "We Found Love." The song spent 10 weeks at the top of the U.S. charts—more than any other single that year.

Rihanna performing on her Loud Tour in Summer 2011.

Rihanna dated L.A. Dodgers baseball player Matt Kemp for most of 2010. At the time, the singer described the handsome outfielder as "my peace."

Rihanna and Matt Kemp enjoy a basketball game in LA in January 2010.

Don't Stop the Music

Rihanna's seventh album hit stores in November 2012, and her Diamonds World Tour kicked off in spring 2013. But music wasn't the only thing on her mind in 2012. The acting bug had caught Rihanna, too.

WORDS OF WISDOM

Rihanna's **motto** in life is "Never a failure, always a lesson." She tattooed those words near the front of her right shoulder. Rihanna had the tattoo inked backwards so she could read it in the mirror!

Hit or Miss

Rihanna hit the high seas—and the big screen—in the spring of 2012. She co-starred in the sci-fi action-adventure film *Battleship*. In the film, Rihanna played a Navy weapons expert named Cora Raikes. Together with her team, Raikes fought aliens who tried to invade Earth.

Rihanna starred alongside Taylor Kitsch (left) and Liam Neeson in *Battleship*.

The film got mixed reviews, but most critics thought *Battleship* was more of a "miss" than a "hit." Rihanna's loyal Navy did not abandon the ship or the new actor, however. Rihanna received the 2012 Teen Choice Award for "Breakout Female" for her role in the film.

Perfect for the Part

Rihanna graced the big screen again in the summer of 2012. She had a small role in the 3D concert film *Katy Perry: Part of Me*. Rihanna–who is good friends with Perry–played herself in the film. Rihanna will also play herself in an upcoming movie called *This Is the End*. In the film, a group of celebrities meet at a party and discover that zombies are on the loose. The creepy comedy–which also stars Seth Rogen, Jonah Hill, James Franco, and Emma Watson–is set to open in June 2013.

Rihanna and friend Katy Perry share a laugh at an awards ceremony.

Styled to Rock

Rihanna hit the small screen in 2012. She appeared on *Styled to Rock*, a British **reality show** in which young designers compete for a chance to dress celebrity rockers. Rihanna worked behind the scenes as the show's executive producer, as well. She has also designed clothing and accessories for Armani. The stylish star hopes to have her own fashion line some day soon.

At Milan Fashion Week in 2008, Rihanna made her catwalk debut.

Sweet Talk

Like many other celebrities, Rihanna has a line of her own fragrances. Reb'l Fleur blends fresh flowers, ripe fruits, and vanilla. Her second perfume, Rebelle, is a sassy but romantic fragrance. Fans can now enjoy Rihanna's scent Nude which was launched in November 2012.

The Reb'l Fleur perfume bottle was designed to look like the high heel of a woman's shoe.

Giving Back

Despite her busy schedule, the generous singer takes time to help those less fortunate than herself. Rihanna started The BELIEVE Foundation in 2006. It is a charity that works to protect and provide for needy children around the world. The foundation helps children get the medicine, school supplies, clothes, and toys they need. Rihanna also records charity songs and performs concerts to raise money for a variety of causes.

Rihanna visits sick children at a New York City hospital, in 2006.

Choose Happiness

Only 25 years old, Rihanna is still growing, as an artist and as a person. Having to do it in front of the world is not always easy. In 2013 she became the center of controversy because she reunited with Chris Brown. She told Oprah Winfrey in a 2012 interview that a role model is "a title of perfection that no one can achieve. I can't say that I'll get it right every time. I wish. I'm a work in progress."

Timeline

1988: Robyn Rihanna Fenty is born on February 20 in Saint Michael, Barbados.

1995: She begins singing at the age of seven but is too shy to perform in public.

2003: Rihanna wins a high-school talent show. She later lands an audition with record producer Evan Rogers, and then moves to the United States to pursue a singing career.

2005: Rihanna auditions for Jay-Z, the head of Def Jam Recordings. She signs a deal to record six albums.

2005: Her debut album, *Music of the Sun*, is released on August 12, followed by her first single, "Pon de Replay."

2006: Rihanna's second studio album, *A Girl Like Me*, is released in the spring and she hits the road for the first time on the Rihanna: Live in Concert Tour.

2006: Rihanna has a cameo role in the cheerleading film *Bring It On: All or Nothing*.

2006: The singer starts a charity called The BELIEVE Foundation.

2007: Rihanna wins a Grammy Award for her hit single, "Umbrella."

2007: She releases her third studio album, *Good Girl Gone Bad* and then kicks off a 16-month tour in the fall.

2009: The singer is assaulted by her boyfriend, R&B star Chris Brown.

2009: Rihanna's edgy fourth album, *Rated R*, is released.

2010: Rihanna begins her Last Girl on Earth Tour to promote the album *Rated R* and releases her fifth album, *Loud*, in November.

2011: The rebel rocker introduces her first women's fragrance, Reb'l Fleur.

2011: Rihanna launches the lively Loud Tour in the summer and releases her sixth album, *Talk That Talk*.

2012: Rihanna stars in the sci-fi action film *Battleship*, and has a cameo in the 3D concert film *Katy Perry: Part of Me*.

2012: She appears in and produces the British fashion reality TV show *Styled to Rock*.

2012: Rihanna's seventh album, *Unapologetic*, hits stores in November.

2013: Her Diamonds World Tour begins in March, and in June she hits the big screen again in a zombie comedy called *This Is the End*.

Glossary

addicted Unable to stop taking drugs or other substances

assaulted Physically attacked or injured by another person

auditioned Tried out for a job or part by giving a short performance

cameo Describes a brief appearance in a film by a well-known performer

collaboration Working together on a project

debut Something that is performed for the first time

demo tape A short recording used to show a musician's talents

elaborate Having many carefully arranged parts and details

headlining Being the main attraction or star of a show

influenced Affected or shaped in an important way

labels Companies that make and sell recorded music

motto Words that express someone's beliefs or ideas about life

peers People who are the same age or social group and are considered equals

probation A period of time during which a person must show good behavior or they will go to jail

promote To share information about a product to help sell it

R&B Rhythm and blues, a form of popular African American music

reality show A show that presents people in real-life situations

signed Hired by a record company

turmoil A time of disturbance or confusion

versatile Able to do many things well

Find Out More

Books

Edwards, Posy. *Rihanna Annual 2013*. Orion, 2012.

Rose, Ella. *Hip-Hop Headliners: Rihanna*. Gareth Stevens Publishing, 2012.

Tieck, Sarah. *Rihanna: Singing Sensation*. Big Buddy Books, 2012.

Websites

Rihanna Now
www.rihannanow.com/
Rihanna's official website

Rihanna Daily
http://rihannadaily.com/
An unofficial fansite

The BELIEVE Foundation
www.believerihanna.com/index.htm
A charity founded by Rihanna

Facebook

www.facebook.com/rihanna

Twitter

https://twitter.com/rihanna

Index

About the Author

Robin Johnson is a freelance author and editor. She has written more than 25 nonfiction children's books, including *Robert Pattinson*, *Taylor Lautner*, and *Katy Perry*. When she isn't working, Robin divides her time fairly evenly between renovating her home with her husband, taking her two sons to hockey practice, and exploring back roads.